HOMESCHOOL PLANNING GUIDE FOR THE UNORGANIZED MOM

MONIQUE BOUTSIV

This book is dedicated to my kids

who have made this journey possible.

TABLE OF CONTENTS

To grab the homeschool planning guide printables to help you get started with your plans, visit:

https://www.livinglifeandlearning.com/the-homeschool-planning-guide

INTRODUCTION

A tear rolled down her cheek and she spoke with a cracked voice as my son's first grade teacher sadly bid us farewell. Mrs. C was every parents dream teacher. She was passionate about her job and loved her students. A day earlier the school principal had informed me that we needed to enroll our son in a different school the next year because we had recently moved. Due to our new address, we were in a different boundary zone which required us to register our son at a different school.

The new school had lower income housing apartments that funnelled into the school. We knew the education was not going to be the same since the old school was one of the top rated schools in the area. So my husband had asked if I wanted to homeschool my son. He had reached out to another homeschooler and felt very confident about the decision. I, however, moved into panic mode because I had never researched it; it had never crossed my mind that we would homeschool our son. I was always an A student and I loved school, so I thought all of our kids would attend school.

We pulled him out at the end of April at the end of his first grade year. This worked well for us, because I had to complete my graduate field work in Alberta, so we all packed up and drove out to Alberta together and spent the summer there and traveling to Seattle. I mimicked school at home with some workbooks that the teacher had recommended. I was pregnant with my second son at this point and was going to be home on maternity leave for a year so we kept my oldest home for second grade.

Because I loved being home with him, and he was enjoying it as well, we continued to homeschool on a year-by-year basis. I never thought we'd homeschool long term but we're heading into our 12th year and it's been a wild ride. I have two boys (18 and 12) and a little princess who is 8.

I graduated with a master's degree in biology, a degree that I have never needed to use since I became a stay at home mother. To help contribute to the family finances, I learned how to code Wordpress websites and started to blog more seriously. I've homeschooled on the road, in a two bedroom apartment, and out of the living room of our current home.

Did I have any clue what I was doing in the beginning? Nope, but I've learned a lot. I have never been a big planner and enjoy flying by the seat of my pants, but when your child asks you on a daily basis, what they have to do today … things need to change.

I've been on both spectrums: loose homeschool plans and super planned out weekly homeschool lessons. I started as a fly by the seat of my pants homeschooler which didn't work out too well. I then went super planned because I was in love with the Charlotte Mason Method and planned out an entire year focused on it. It didn't last a term and all my plans went out the window. I'm happy to say that I've found my happy place. It falls somewhere in between, with a great yearly overall plan and a flexible weekly plan in place that can be changed accordingly. Did it happen overnight? Nope, it definitely took some trial and error but it's something that every mom has to figure out for herself. Are you that super type A planner with sticky notes and washi tape and everything planned out for the year or are you the fly by the seat of your pants mom who follows those rabbit trails where ever they lead?

I'm not one to plan out every hour of my day, I like having the kids take the lead so a timed daily schedule would never fly in our house. Don't be put off when I say homeschool plans, it can be a set of overall goals or planned down to the hour. Your personality and homeschool method will contribute to what your homeschool plans look like but you never have to do anything you don't want to.

I can get you started with everything you need to start homeschool planning but remember it's going to take some work. By the time we are finished, you'll have a set of plans ready to get started with your homeschool whether you plan for the full year or for just a few weeks.

CHAPTER 1

WHAT YOU NEED TO KNOW
BEFORE YOU GET STARTED

WHY HOMESCHOOL

We enjoy homeschooling because it provides us with more family time and with my husband's work hours, he would never see them if they were in school. It's something that I never knew I wanted until we were called to homeschool our oldest. He was an introvert and happy to come home. However, I also know that not everyone homeschools for the same reasons. It may not be so easy for different families. It may be that the school system had failed you and your child or there could have been bullying issues. Homeschooling may have been a last resort and you were thrown into it. It may be something that you knew you were going to do from the moment you gave birth or it may have been something you thought you'd only do for one term and here you are. You can homeschool for religious reasons, or you weren't happy with your child's circle of influence, or the education system in your school district was lacking. If you are able to provide a better education than your school can or you want to be able to have that time with your family, homeschooling can be an option for you. You may have wanted to create your own schedule and travel across the country in an RV or attend swimming competitions when needed. Homeschooling allows you to be masters of your own schedules. Whatever, the reason, the homeschool journey is not an easy one but by having plans in place, is one component that you won't need to worry about again. It's one less thing to worry about once it's set up and it's one less thing to think about when you start your busy day.

Before you jump into teaching

If you're brand new to homeschooling, likely your first concern is around what you will use to teach, how you will teach your child, or what can you buy to help you homeschool. Instead of focusing on the curriculum, the plans or the budget, the first thing you should focus on is you. Realize that you will be transitioning into the role of your child's teacher. I'm sure you've had lovely daydreams of your family sitting around the kitchen table hanging onto every word that you speak. The reality is that homeschooling can be chaotic and hard. Your baby may be crying on your hip, most days the toddler will dump out his sensory rice bin onto the floor, and more than once your 1st grader will refuse to do her math. Get used to it.

There will be good days and bad days but if you know why you're homeschooling, this will push you through on those bad days. It will help keep you moving forward. When those math meltdowns happen or when your child vows never to learn how to spell, you will keep on going.

Research

Do your due diligence and research the homeschool requirements for your state or province. This varies greatly and is beyond the scope of this book. You may need to keep transcripts, grades, attendance and number of hours of school completed. You may also have to complete standardized tests or reports required by your state or province.

At the time of this book, I will tell you that in Ontario, Canada, if your child was in public school, you are required to file a letter of intent with your school board. There is no record keeping or testing that is required. Parents are able to plan their own curriculum and are not held accountable by anyone. This also means we don't receive any funding. I know parents who homeschool in Alberta get funding from the government so research what is offered in your area. As I look ahead to college and university for my oldest, record keeping in the high school years is a huge benefit as they'll want transcripts and a portfolio. Depending on his career path, he may also need to take the SATs. Get familiar with the laws and requirements for your area of residence.

Get your family on board

I was an unexpected homeschooler, so my husband had to get me on board with homeschooling. It's important to discuss this as a family. My oldest son was an introvert and happy to come home for school. I know some moms have to convince their husband or children that it's a good idea to homeschool. If your spouse or child is completely against homeschooling, consider homeschooling for a trial period, or have some deep discussions about the pros and cons and let him voice his concerns to see how they can be addressed and if a compromise can be reached.

Speak with your children. If they've attended public school, they may be worried about losing their friends. Homeschoolers have plenty of opportunities to make friends, it just takes more effort to seek out those opportunities. There are homeschool co-ops, play groups and local groups that you can join to make friends and connect with other families.

Set your expectations aside

If you jump into homeschooling with huge expectations, you'll only be let down. I know I started out envisioning homeschooling as a family who cuddles on the couch doing school work, but, that is not always the case. The kids are fighting, they don't want to do their school work and the toddler has created a huge mess when you were distracted by the older children. If you're homeschooling because your child was having trouble at school, don't expect to have trouble from the start, you never know the changes that may occur once you bring your child home so don't set them too low either. Life is going to happen. I prefer to set goals rather than expectations and we'll get into that later.

Set some time to deschool

If you're pulling your child out of school, let them have a deschooling period. A time to discover what it is that they love or what they'd like to learn about. They have an opportunity to provide input into their education now and it would be a great time to discuss their desires. This means you don't have to hit the books hard if they are just coming out of school. I know there's always the mad dash to seek and acquire curriculum, but also give your child a chance to have a say in what they learn. Who says you have to start with ancient history if your child is extremely interested in the two world wars?

Give yourself grace

You are not perfect. You are not supposed to be. Give yourself grace and permission to mess up, make mistakes, learn from them, and have chocolate parties. Because being a mother is hard, a homeschooling mother also has the added responsibility of their child's education.

WHAT IS MY CHILD'S LEARNING STYLE?

Before you start planning out your curriculum, it would be a wise move to determine your child's learning style. You may also want to consider your preferred learning styles.

You could skip this step, but it probably won't end well and there may be lots of tears involved, including your own. I'm speaking here from experience. It's likely that you are one specific type of learner and you're most likely going to teach your child that way as well. I'm an auditory learner so I like to teach using auditory methods, this really doesn't work for my visual learner.

Really observe your child, what do they like to do, what are their favorite activities? How do they respond best to you? Do they prefer to talk things out, can they remember things that they are told rather that what they see? Do they remember details after seeing things only once? Do they do best with hands-on experiences?

Auditory Learners

If your child can easily remember oral instructions, and responds well to your requests or directions, they are more likely auditory learners. They love listening to you read, they may read slowly to themselves, they are natural listeners, and do well working through ideas via discussions rather than written word. They may talk your ear off and can express themselves well verbally.

Kinaesthetic Learners

If your child learns through movement or by "doing" then you have a kinaesthetic learner. These children may fidget or move as they are speaking or listening to you. They need frequent study breaks and they learn best while completing hands-on tasks such as building with blocks or Legos, creating arts and crafts, and completing science experiments.

Visual Learners

Visual learners remember what they see and have a wonderful sense of direction. They think in pictures and have difficulty with oral instruction. They learn best using drawing as a tool, mind maps and graphic organizers. They love picture books and can remember great visual details while forgetting verbal instructions.

What kind of learner do you have? It's not always clear cut because it is possible that children don't fit into a specific mould but may draw from two or more of these characteristics. Only you will be able to tell as their parent.

Knowing this will allow you to teach to their strengths, but you also want to work on their weaknesses, as well. This will give them a variety of tools to help them learn independently.

Action tasks

• Determine your child's learning style.

WHICH HOMECHOOOL METHOD WILL YOU CHOOSE?

Homeschool planning can look very different depending on the method of homeschooling you'll choose to use with your family. When I first started homeschooling my son, I followed the school at home method because I wasn't even aware there were different options. I used the workbooks that his teacher recommended and we did similar work to what he completed at school because that's what I knew. When I started reading about different methods I was completely drawn to the Charlotte Mason method and planned out his entire 2nd grade year using this same method. Well, after 3 months, I relinquished and decided that it didn't work well for my son. We then discovered lapbooks and that transformed our homeschool. We do a lot of written narration using lapbooks, small booklets for capturing what they've learned, and notebooking pages, pages with writing lines and space to draw pictures and diagrams. It was more relaxed and allowed my son to express what he learned using pictures. As a visual learner, this worked really well with him. Just know that there are options when it comes to homeschool methods.

School at Home

This follows the more traditional path of classroom learning by using textbooks, testing with multiple choice or fill in the blank answers. You complete the next thing in the book and you would use the same principle for each of your subjects.

Charlotte Mason education

Charlotte Mason was an educator from Britain at the start of the twentieth century who believed in teaching the whole child. This method uses living books instead of textbooks, encourages a lot of outdoor time with nature study, as well as emphasizes the arts with artists and composer studies. For language arts, they believe in copywriting and narration from classical pieces of writing. Habit training and creating routines for the child is important.

Classical education

The classical education model believes in three stages of learning:

Grammar – grade 1-4

Logic – grade 5-8

Rhetoric – grade 9-12

Grammar stage focuses on absorbing new knowledge through memorization, rules and expanding their vocabulary.

Logic stage is where students start to reason and make connections with what they've learned in the previous stage. This also means they begin to ask questions and may become more argumentative to challenge others.

The rhetoric stage teaches the child to communicate in more affective and articulate manner and study from primary sources. Classical education believes in studying the classical languages first like Latin or Greek.

Montessori education

The Montessori Method focuses on the development of the child as an individual person full of a natural curiosity. The idea is to nurture this curiosity during the early years (0-6 years old) by providing the right opportunities to learn. Maria Montessori insisted that children were mature individuals capable of learning things on their own because of their natural curiosity. Teachers are to have a supportive role and provide an environment conducive to their learning at a level appropriate for them. The premise of the Montessori Method uses materials that are highly kinaesthetic since children learn with all of their senses. Activities are grouped by age and skill. The focuses are on learning practical life skills and improve coordination. They pour liquids and food into other containers, play with buckles, zippers, and buttons, and clean tabletops. They learn where their place in the world is through geography and science. Reading starts with learning the alphabet with a movable alphabet and/or sandpaper letters.

Unschooling

John Holt, first used the term in the 1970's, he believed that children would learn naturally when they were ready to do so. As long as a supportive environment was in place, learning would take place according to the child's interest. He felt that the school environment was unnatural and that children should not be pushed to learn things they didn't wish to. Unschooling parents believe that the child will learn things at their own pace. In the beginning, it may appear as though unschooling students are behind since they do not teach formal reading or math but the child learns through more natural means when they are ready to do so.

There is no teaching on the parent's part, no curriculum, or classes unless the child requests them. The parent's role is to provide learning opportunities. You may take a trip to a butterfly conservatory, raise caterpillars, leave out books or videos, but it is up to the child to delve into the material when they are ready to show an interest.

Unit studies

It is the study of a topic or theme using numerous school subjects. For example, if we were studying butterflies, you would incorporate their history, geography - where they are found, math - count butterflies in your backyard, and science - raise caterpillars. Your homeschool revolves around one theme to unite all your studies. Unit studies are great for families that want to spend time studying together. You can design or select activities that are appropriate for the ages of your children. That way you can teach your fourth grader and seventh grader together but may have specific requirements from each. You could require a written summary and drawing from your fourth grader and ask your seventh grader to research a related topic and write an essay on that topic.

Online Learning

You may use an online program or your child may take online classes through your school district or other courses. This means you'd have to follow their schedule and ensure that your school fits around their timeline and depending on if they have to attend live sessions.

Eclectic homeschoolers are those who don't identify with one method but may pull bits from one or another method to find something that works for their family. You may find that you like to teach math with a textbook but want to approach science in an unschooling manner.

WHAT IS YOUR HOMESCHOOL BUDGET?

The beauty of homeschooling is that it can cost as much or as little as you'd like. I do not get any funding for my homeschool so everything I purchase is out of pocket. However, if you're in a state/province that provides funding, you'll have more money to play with in your studies.

What do you need to factor in?

- Homeschool curriculum
- School supplies
- Computer
- Printer
- Extra-curricular activities
- Co-op classes
- Online classes
- Special equipment ie Microscopes, slides

The second year, I discovered all of these homeschool resources I went a little crazy and became a curriculum junkie. That year I spent $500 on books for my only child who was in grade 2. Last year, for books, I spent less than $100 with three kids because I had curriculum from my oldest child that I could use with my younger son. So if you have children who learn in a similar way, you may consider holding onto your curriculum for them. I was able to borrow my teen's science curriculum, microscope and slides and split a writing curriculum with another mom. I know mothers who homeschool very frugally and only use free resources. What you save in money you may have to give up in time. You don't have everything ready to go in a box, you have to search for what you need or create it yourself. If you think that you have to spend thousands of dollars to homeschool, you don't, and there are definitely ways to save on curriculum which I'll go into later.

To grab the homeschool planning guide printables to help you get started with your plans, visit:

https://www.livinglifeandlearning.com/the-homeschool-planning-guide

DOES YOUR HOMESCHOOL HAVE A MISSION STATEMENT?

Now that you have a handle on your child's learning style, you can start thinking of a homeschool mission statement. Whether you're new to homeschooling or a veteran, consider giving your homeschool a mission statement. What is the reason you are homeschooling? Have you really thought about this? Put it into writing so that it will serve as a reminder to everyone in your homeschool.

No, your homeschool won't fall apart if you don't have one, but it's great to start planning your homeschool year by evaluating the purpose of your homeschool.

Why are you homeschooling? What skills or issues will you be addressing this year and what will be a priority in your homeschool. Thinking through these questions will give you a clear path to set your homeschool on.

When days are tough and you feel like you want to throw in the towel, a glance at your mission statement will give you a much needed reminder of why you started this crazy adventure in the first place. Let's face it we all have those days.

A mission statement will give your homeschool a path to strive for even on those tough days when it seems that no one is listening or when no one wants to do any work or when you feel like throwing the math book across the room.

All businesses create mission statements for their place of work and you are doing serious work by taking on your children's education. Start out right,create your mission statement today, print it out, and place it where you and the family can read it as needed.

Action Tasks

- Create a mission statement for your homeschool.
- Print it out and place in a spot that is readily visible.

CHAPTER 2

DON'T GET OVERWHELMED WITH HOMESCHOOL CURRICULUM

HOW TO CHOOSE THE BEST HOMESCHOOL CURRICULUM

You are now responsible for your child's education, you feel a huge weight on your shoulders. You want to find the best curriculum for your child but you also need to balance it with your budget. Things can be overwhelming in the beginning because of the huge selection of homeschool curricula available but you have to remember to breath, take things slowly, and don't panic. You want to ensure that you're covering your bases but you know that you won't have the time or money to do every single thing that you've fallen in love with. Now you'll need to decide on the best homeschool curriculum for your family.

Does it match your child's learning style?

Once you've discovered your child's learning style, it's important to find curriculum that will cater or teach to their strengths. If you found a great history curriculum with audio CDs, your visual learner might not be so excited about it but your auditory learner would be totally on board with that. You'll want to ensure that you've also incorporated drawing, maps and other activities to make it more appealing to your visual learner. Your kinaesthetic learner will need plenty of manipulatives and hands-on activities to make their curriculum work for them.

Does it fit your budget?

A curriculum that requires you to spend three months' worth of savings, better be one awesome curriculum. If you've dished out money on curriculum you're not using or it isn't a right fit, it will leave a sour feeling in your homeschool if you force yourself to use it. Be realistic about your budget and also about the curriculum, do you absolutely need it or can you find a cheaper alternative?

Will your child love it?

They may not love everything you do in your homeschool but it's a great idea to get your child involved in their homeschool planning. Do they have a preference for certain types of material like computer based programs or workbooks? Ask them what topics they'd like to study and incorporate it into their school. Which period of history would they like to study? If it's the middle ages, then fine, who said you had to start with the ancients anyways? You don't have to be a stickler for the rules or follow what you think everyone else is doing, your child will thank you.

Does it align with your goals for the year?

Well, yes that awesome science curriculum is on sale but is that what you were planning to teach this year? Do you mind having it sit on the shelf for a year? What are your goals for your child this year and what can you use to teach them? Is there a focus on literature or perhaps you'd like to teach more independence. Will this allow that to happen? Ask these questions to yourself as you are looking at curriculum and making that final choice.

Do you have time to use it?

Yes, you might love to use all three of these wonderful studies but do you have enough time? You do need to sleep you know. You can buy tons of curriculum but there's no use cramming it into a tight schedule because it will be tossed aside when time is limited.

There is no such thing as the perfect curriculum. Stop chasing it. You can spend all year planning for the best curriculum and still have it fizzle with your child. You won't know for sure until you get it in your hands and use it with your child. Can you picture yourself using it and enjoying it? If you prefer a script with daily lessons plans then those unit studies where you pick and create your own lessons won't work for you. Know yourself, know what you can accomplish, and know your limits.

Action Tasks

- List your child's/childrens' names with each subject and fill in the curriculum you'd like to use for each child.

HOW TO SAVE MONEY ON HOMESCHOOL CURRICULUM

If you have multiple children working at different grade levels, homeschooling can get expensive. You've decided to take on the responsibility of your child's education and now that you've made that huge decision, can you afford to give them the curriculum you long to use? We've discussed the need to examine your budget so you can make wise purchasing choices. Now let's go through other ways we can help keep that budget down.

Do your research

Don't make any impulse purchases but instead take the time to look into what you will need for each child. What areas do they struggle in and what areas would you like to concentrate on? Go through and make a list of curricula that you'd like to look into. I then make a list and research the heck out of it. I read online reviews. I price the items for both new and used items from different vendors. I keep a record of everything so that when I'm looking for curriculum the next year for another child, I don't have to go through the whole process again.

Once you've completed your research and determined if it will be a good fit, then you can go ahead and think about purchasing the item.

Don't believe the hype

I know I get excited when I hear about a new curriculum that people are buzzing about. I read the positive reviews from people who have used the books and then I race out to buy it and find out that it's just not a great fit for our family. It doesn't jive with my teaching style or my child's learning style so it gets tossed aside and sits on my shelf collecting dust. Again, had I taken the time to research, read online reviews, asked in the forums or Facebook groups, or discussed it with local friends then I may have passed on the item and saved myself that money.

There are no greener pastures

Sometimes, I examine what's working for us and think, "what if we used this curriculum instead? Maybe it would be better." I change things up and then find that it just doesn't work, or so and so loved this so I have to try it because my kids are missing out. Be confident that you've done the best job at choosing the right items for your family. Only you will know what works, don't worry about what others are doing and focus on the needs of your family.

Buy used curriculum

I'll go into more detail in the next section but you don't have to buy all of your books new, you can buy them used, and save a ton of money. This will take some time and planning but it will allow you to save money on books. You'll need to make a list of the things you want and keep an eye out for them. You'll have more difficulty finding less common curriculum.

Barter your services

If you're able to teach music lessons and someone else rocks at science, how about swapping lessons for your children? You could also start your own homeschool co-op in your home. Get creative and find opportunities for your children without feeling as though you're missing out on all the good stuff.

HOW TO BUY AND SELL USED HOMESCHOOL CURRICULUM

Once you start to figure out what you want to use for your child's homeschool curriculum you may be hit with sticker shock. How can you afford to homeschool your child? If you're dedicated to using that awesome, but pricey, homeschool curriculum then you'll need to see if you can purchase it used. This will save you tons and once you're done with it, you can probably turn around and sell it to someone else for a reasonable price.

By selling your old curriculum, you can use that money to purchase new curriculum or extra-curricular activities.

Some of my favorite places to buy used homeschool books:

- EBay
- Craigslist/Kijiji
- Veg Source
- Homeschool Classifieds
- Homeschool Reviews
- The Well-Trained Mind Forums
- Local book stores

Get yourself set up so that you're ready to buy and sell curriculum.

Set up a Paypal account

This is the first step you need to take because it may take some time to set up. I linked my Paypal account to my bank account so I can easily add money and make withdrawals into the account. Paypal also protects buyers, so if there are any issues with not receiving your purchases you can easily file a claim within a certain period of time. As a seller, you want to ensure that your shipment is tracked so that you can see that is delivered to the correct address to protect yourself from wrongful claims.

Check the ratings

I like to buy items through systems that have a rating system like eBay and the Well-Trained Mind Forums so you can see the history of the buyer or seller. In my eight years of homeschooling, I only had one issue with a seller. I didn't receive my product after payment and the seller ignored all of my emails and communication so I was able to dispute the purchase with Paypal and got my money refunded.

Check out the competition

If it is a popular curriculum, there may be a lot of sellers selling the same material, those items will have a lower resale value. Use this information to adjust your expectations around the value of your curriculum.

What condition is your book in?

Books that are in a rough state or not as crisp will fetch a lower price. Be sure to list what state your books are in or be sure to ask about the condition of books before you make a purchase. State or ask if there's writing in workbooks or if are there any pages missing. Take pictures of the book before you sell them, you'll always get questions about the condition of your books, so have them ready.

How much is shipping?

Calculate shipping before you list your items for sale so that you can easily respond to questions. When making a purchase, make sure you've asked if the price includes shipping or not. If you have a scale at home, it would save you time, otherwise you'll need to get your parcels priced at the postal office.

What else does the curriculum need?

You may get questions pertaining to the curriculum, such as: does it include the teacher's manual or do you need a student workbook? Keep track of the supporting material that may be required or optional. This will help you answer any questions you may get. As a buyer, you'll want to ask those questions, does it include the teacher's manual, can the curriculum be used without it, and so on.

Action Tasks

- Set up a Paypal account.
- Decide which books you'd like to buy or sell.

HOW TO KEEP TRACK OF YOUR HOMESCHOOL CURRICULUM TO SAVE MONEY

Are you a curriculum junkie? My second year of homeschooling I went crazy after I discovered there was all this homeschool curriculum out there. I was amazed to find that there were so many options for each subject. I was like a kid in a candy store every time I received a new homeschool catalogue in the mail. However, there are only so many hours in a day, and you can't get through it all, no matter how hard you try.

I organize all of my books by subject and then any that are not appropriate for me to use right now I move to my second floor closet. Books that I need stay downstairs in my living room, where I homeschool, on the book shelves if they'll be used within the year, or if they're a resource book, so they are readily available.

I like to keep a running list of the curriculum that I have because you may forget what you have tucked away in that box in the basement. I've put away all of my early elementary resources because I didn't need them with my two boys. If I didn't organize my books, I'd have to go through my boxes to see what I have to use with my daughter. However, since I've kept a file of my books, I can take a peek quickly and know what I still need to purchase for the upcoming year.

It's also a great idea to note what format you have (a book or digital file), if you've consumed the workbook, or do you need a teacher's manual.

It's so much easier to do this in the beginning as you start to build up your curriculum library, get started now.

Action Tasks

- Make a record of all the homeschool curriculum you own.
- List the subject, name, required/optional materials, format, and location.

WHY YOU SHOULD DITCH THE HOMESCHOOL CURRICULUM

Does your child have a particular hobby or interest that they've asked you about? Why don't you incorporate it into your homeschool? Sometimes there will be a lack of curriculum that you need or a lack of funds. However, why should that stop you from teaching your child what they desire?

After all this homeschool curriculum talk, you must think I'm crazy when I say it is fine to ditch that homeschool curriculum. Yes, I said it. You don't need the best, most popular homeschool curriculum out there on the market, you can create your own. In the early elementary years, I do this for science as I'm not particularly fond of any science curriculum at this stage. I asked my kids what they'd like to learn about and created our own studies using library books, documentaries and notebooking pages to document what my child has learned.

Follow their interests

You can create interest-led or unit studies based on what your child wants to learn. Imagine how powerful and excited your child will feel as they help shape their homeschooling journey and they'll truly love what they're learning. I'm not saying you need to ditch curriculum altogether but maybe you could start with one subject. I like doing this with science and history because it's easy to study a specific topic and they're so many options to choose from.

This is easier to do if you feel confident in teaching that subject. I'm a science graduate and I love teaching science because it's interesting and I'm confident in my abilities to do so. But if you're not so confident, it will only take more research on your part and require more planning. My weakness is in language arts so I use a curriculum for those subjects that I need help with. No one said you had to ditch everything at once. Do what you are comfortable with and so you don't get in over your head.

Create a lifelong learner

Homeschooling doesn't have to be like school at home. I think everyone who leaves public school mimics school at home for the first year. But you begin to break free from that education model and realize that learning can take place in many shapes and forms. My goal is to create a lifelong learner, someone who thoroughly enjoys learning new things and doesn't stop when school is over. We discovered lapbooks and notebooking which caused me to let go of the traditional fill in the blank, multiple choice and short answer test models that can easily kill the love of learning.

You begin to realize that you can truly do this and you can do a great job like any other teacher out there as long as you have a solid plan and resources in place. It's ok if you don't know all of the answers, but look up the answers with your child and teach them how to research and ask even more questions.

Action Tasks

- Decide on a topic and create your first interest-led study.

HOW TO CREATE A READING LIST

Books are what drive the imagination and I love it when the kids get into a series of books, it's wonderful to watch them jump into a new world. The rule in our house is that if the movie has a book, it must be read first before we watch the movies. We're currently working our way through the Chronicles of Narnia with my younger son. My oldest has read all of them already; it was one of our favorite series.

I love creating reading lists for my kids because I look forward to all the books they'll get to enjoy. It also helps you stay organized if you need to order them from the library so you're not scrambling for book titles last minute. You'll learn more about using the library effectively later on.

Find books at the correct reading level

Ensure that you are reading with your child daily, this will give them more practice and it will become incorporated into their routine. Have your child read aloud to you so you know what words they have trouble with and what reading level they are at. My boys first started reading Bob books and then moved to Dr. Seuss books for their early readers and they loved them.

If the book is too difficult your child may get frustrated, so stick to books that are at/below their reading level. This makes reading a pleasant experience and helps build up their confidence which can be an issue with some children. For your avid readers, you can obviously increase the level of difficulty to stretch them and encourage them to read more difficult books. I encourage you to review these books first to ensure that your child is emotionally ready to read "older" books that may contain more mature themes or ideas. I know I don't like to read about murder and killings early on and you'll have to be the judge of that with your child for when they're ready to deal with more complicated issues.

I like to have my child read aloud to me because although they may read books well, I want them to have the pronunciation correct as well and there is no way to gauge that until I hear them read.

How to find good books to read

Ask your librarian, they are the best resource for book suggestions, I love them. Our library also has different list resources that they use to recommend books for children. I enjoy these lists as I prefer to stick with the classics with great literature then the fluff that they produce to get children to read about farting or underwear.

If we like a book, for example, Charlie and the Chocolate Factory, then we'll try another one of the author's books as well. I like looking at the suggestions at the bottom of Amazon listings to see what other books are similar to the one you just read to get ideas for new books. Use higher level reading books for read alouds.

For your read alouds, choose books that are at a higher level of reading to expose your child to new vocabulary. Read daily and you will have a lifelong reader in your household. Make reading fun and don't treat it as a chore. I love snuggling on my couch with my kids and a good book that we all enjoy. Now that they're getting older, we're going through books for a second time as I read books to my younger children, but my older son often likes to sit in and listen because he remembers those books as well.

Action tasks

- Decide what books each of your children will read.
- Decide what books you'll read aloud together.

HOW TO USE THE LIBRARY EFFECTIVELY IN YOUR HOMESCHOOL

Homeschooling can get very expensive when you add up all the books for each subject, which is worst if you have more than one child at home. One of the ways to offset those costs is to use the library as often as you can. We've planned our homeschool schedule but do you have a library schedule?

We all do it, the library can get awfully expensive if you don't get your books renewed on time, or if they're not returned by the due date, or sometimes they get damaged or lost and you have to spend a ridiculous amount of money to replace it with their added admin fee. It can be a nightmare and shun you from using the library.

This is why I like to have my reading list ready for the year because sometimes books are not available when you need them and I can just jump down to the next book on the list and have no worries about missing out on the first book.

Keep track of renewal dates

Use a planner or an online calendar that sends you a reminder. The likelihood that you'll remember it when those two or three weeks are up is not going to happen. You have 30 books out and at $0.10 a day for each book, things add up quickly. I use the Google Calendar app on my phone to add the date and it notifies me when that time comes by way of an alarm so I can't miss it.

Keep books separate

I keep all the library books in one area and my own personal books in another. We try to keep library books separated from our own books because when it's time to head out to the library and you're looking for that one book, it becomes extremely elusive. It hides among your books and camouflages itself making it impossible to find. I do this to maintain my sanity on library days. I also know that I have to be more careful around the library books while my own get tossed around.

No liquids near books

That is a hard rule that I stick to, nothing hurts me more than spilling something on one of those huge hardcover books that cost an arm and a leg to replace. Not happening here. Books stay in the living room or bedroom and there are no liquids in those rooms while they are reading. I love that they can enjoy books that we can't afford to purchase but your kids also have to know how to properly handle the books as well. No rough play and no chewing on them, yes, I've had to utter those words to my preschooler.

Proper transportation

We take out about 25 books each time we are at the library, so I use a huge plastic reusable shopping bag but whatever you use make sure it is waterproof. I couldn't find my regular reusable shopping bag one time and opted for a flimsy bag, well unbeknownst to me, my husband had spilled some tea in the truck and there goes that brand new essential oil book. So heartbreaking when you have to pay for a brand new book and you can't take the old one because it's ruined. Ugh.

Reduce the videos

DVDs or other electronics cost more to replace and cost more in fines if they're late. I do not take these out anymore unless it's something I can't find online or on Netflix. I usually end up with scratched up DVDs and then the kids are upset it doesn't work and then I have to pay for it because I forgot to renew it after the 1 week mark. Therefore, we just don't do library DVDs anymore, it's not worth the headache.

Inter-library loan

Does your library have a inter library loan system? I love this. If your system of libraries doesn't have the book you need, you can request it through the ILL system. If they are able to locate it at another library they will ship the book to your library for you. This has saved me when I've really wanted to read a book and it's not available at our library which is small. Best thing ever, but it does take some time to get your book and then you usually can't renew it, at least at my library, so plan accordingly.

Make Suggestions

If you need a new book, make a suggestion for the library to purchase it and then you'll be first in line to get it once it comes in. It never hurts to ask. I've done this several times and have been delighted with how quick they respond.

CHAPTER 3

HOW TO CREATE A
HOMESCHOOL SCHEDULE

MAKE TIME TO PLAN FOR YOUR HOMESCHOOL

Yes, to start your homeschooling year on the right foot, you'll first need to make the time to plan. I received an email from a reader who asked, "How can I find the time to plan with a newborn of 6 weeks, preschooler, kindergartner and a gifted student?" As she wrote the email she stated that her kids were currently on electronics and that she was trying to get the baby to sleep. Her biggest fear was that she'd start the school year with nothing planned and with the kids stuck on their electronics.

I know when we think of homeschooling, you think you have to have everything planned out for the entire year, however, you actually only need to be one day ahead of your student. Of course, it will save your sanity if you have a few weeks planned instead.

My first advice is to start small. Start with one subject or start with just one child. For me, for some reason I come up with the best ideas when I'm on my phone. I like to start planning in Evernote, I list each of my children and subjects and fill this in as I go. Evernote syncs to all of my devices and the computer. When I get on my computer to sit down I have a pretty good idea of what I need to research. I have a plan and I'm not wondering around aimlessly and losing myself on homeschooling sites or online book stores.

I know I can spend hours reading curriculum reviews, heading to Facebook groups to seek advice, and reading comments on what other families used, but to be time efficient you need to be laser focused or you'll get that shiny object syndrome and won't get anything done.

When should you start planning for the next year?

In the spring

For those that are already homeschooling, the best time to start homeschool planning is in the spring. Unless you're like me, I like to start thinking about things in January. By now you are almost finished your school year and should already have a good idea of what is working or not working in your homeschool. If it's working then it's likely that you'll use the next level in the book series for the next year. If it's not, then you may want to look at alternative options.

This is the best time because spring is when homeschooling conference season may be starting in your area. My local conference is always at the end of April. If you're planning on going, it's always a great idea to plan ahead and know what to be on the lookout for. Conferences always have vendor tables, which allow you to see materials in person and ask questions of the vendors. Having a plan ensures that you don't end up with expensive impulse purchases. If you attend a conference with no plan, you may regret your purchases later.

Summer planning

We homeschool year round so I don't have to get things ready until September which means I do my planning in August. We officially start the next school year in September but if we're ahead in our program we'll just continue on in the summer, there's no reason to wait. I like to enjoy my short break in July and my lighter homeschool schedule, so that the boys have lots of outdoor time. However, in August I'm in full planning mode and want to have everything ordered so they'll arrive by the first week of September.

This works for me because I can do it a little at a time and slowly work through it and not be pressured with homeschooling a full-time schedule while trying to plan for the next year.

Plan as you go

Start small, don't feel as though you have to plan out the entire year. Plan out a month or a term (3 months) ahead. Things may change and curriculum may get tossed. You only need to be a day or preferably a week ahead of your child. If you're not a planner or scared of the whole concept of planning, go this route and see if it eases your fears. You just need to get started. Book lists help you stay organized for those library visits, so planning does help, but it shouldn't be overwhelming.

We're mothers and we're all busy, but if you have time to watch TV, or read or exercise, make some time to plan for your homeschool, and it doesn't have to be the whole shebang. Start small and add to it as you can. It doesn't have to be perfect but it will help you progress through the year so you can see if you're on track or if you need to pick things up.

Action Tasks

• Decide when and where you'll set aside some time to plan for your homeschool year, even if it's 15 minutes a day.

WHAT ARE YOUR HOMESCHOOL GOALS?

You won't go anywhere if you don't have a direction of where you are heading. If you don't have a goal for your child or your family, making final decisions can be difficult because you don't know your end goal. When you think about your homeschool year, have you set goals for each of your children? If you can set homeschool goals for your child, this will help you figure out the right curriculum for your homeschool. If your child is struggling in a subject, you'll know you to set aside a bit more time for this subject.

When it comes down to two curriculum choices, you can use your goals to help make your decision. If one of them is to provide more hands-on activities for your child then the text book may not be the choice for you now. If your goal is to get your child reading fluently, then maybe you want to spend more time selecting books he'll like to read and playing different reading or spelling games. Setting family goals and goals for yourself as a teacher can help drive you through those long and hard days as you work toward a goal.

Academic goals

What would you like your child to get out of homeschooling this year? What skills would you like to focus on? What subjects would really interest him?

My son would love to learn about rockets for science so how about looking into a physical science curriculum with lots of hands on activities. So his goal would be to build his own rocket ship. If your daughter would love to read the Narnia books, you could try a unit study to stretch things out and really jump deep into the books.

If your goal is for your child to read, you'll know that your focus will be on reading fluency. How about finding some fun new readers, sight word games and reading resources to make learning fun. There are some wonderful online games as well.

If your child needs to learn independence, then a teacher intensive curriculum may not be the answer.

Character goals

Are there any issues that you need to address as a parent? Do we need to work on fostering sibling love or sharing? Make a list of character traits you'd like to work on this year with tasks and ideas to implement them as well. Learning doesn't have to be confined to school, character development can take place when you visit your friends, attend extracurricular activities, or volunteer.

Personal goals

Don't be afraid to ask your child, do they want to learn the piano or take up a new sport? Perhaps they'd like to read x number of books this year. Maybe they'd like to learn to knit or crochet, ask them what interests them and how you can help them achieve their own goals and put it in writing. Then ask them how they will achieve it and determine ways or tasks that will help them get closer to the end result.

Some examples to get your started include: reading 10 chapter books, to learn a second language, learn to build their own radio, create jewelry to be able to sell them, create their own blog about video games or another passion.

Action tasks

• Set goals for your family, yourself and each child.

WHAT EXTRACURRICULAR ACTIVITIES WILL YOUR CHILD LOVE?

I've given tips on how to create our homeschool schedule but what have you filled it with? What extracurricular activities would your child love? We've discussed goals and schedules but you also need to round out your schedule with some extracurricular activities.

Sports

Does your child love sports? Any kind of team sports like soccer or baseball is a great way to stay social and physically active for your kids. One of my boys loves being around other kids his age plus he's competitive so he gravitates towards team sports.

My daughter is only four, but she's now in gymnastic classes and she loves it. It's a wonderfully small homeschool class and while they're building new skills, they're having a lot of fun doing it, too. She's been sick this past week but would never think of missing a gymnastics class. The local YMCA also has several sports options that are drop in programs with a variety of sports.

Martial arts

Although I guess this activity could go under sports, I consider it more for personal development. You are physically active but it's up to you to work towards your goal yourself. My son who does not love team sports was more willing to try judo. His homeschool friend was in it and he wanted to join him. It turned out to be great way to learn about following directions, gross motor coordination, and exercise.

He's a clumsy one, so our goal was to help him get more coordinated and he had fun doing it. They played a lot of wonderful games, and since it was a big class he was also able to build team skills. My younger son has been in a recreational karate class and we've decided to put him into Judo for the new school year which involves a bit more one-on-one work.

Arts

If you don't have a sports lover, how about catering to their creative side with art or dance? In our city, we have a lot of options for art classes and art lessons with other homeschooling families. There's also a variety of dance classes held at our local community centre that is very budget friendly, however, if you have a serious dancer, you'd probably want to go with a dance school or academy as they can get them to the competitive level. The community center offers classes for very reasonable prices so it's a great way to test a new interest before committing yourself to more serious options.

Swimming

We consider swimming a life skill; it's necessary for survival, particularly if you're near water. This is a non-negotiable activity that our whole family does and it's a great way to spend family together while being active.

4H

Classes will vary by location but can include anything from quilting, dairy, camping, knitting and animals. If there's someone available to teach then it can be a class. Costs are usually very reasonable.

Computers

Computers are here to stay, perhaps you have a techy child who would love to learn how to code and design games. They're not going anywhere so you might as well embrace it. My child is learning HTML and CSS through Code Academy and it's free. I hope to employ him to do some work for me once he's done. There are often computer camps or perhaps they may be into robotics, we have a local Lego robotics team that meets up weekly to prepare for the robotic competition.

Music

For those that are musically impaired, like me, you may need to outsource music lessons to others. Ask around to see where other homeschoolers are taking lessons. Check out the local university and see if there are music students who offer lessons which would be more budget friendly than music schools. We use an online program to teach my son music with his keyboard because private lessons are out of the budget for us now.

Co-op

If you haven't found anything that would work for your child or that is in your budget, considering starting your own co-op. You never know what skills other parents may be able to offer your child. You could teach their children while they teach yours a new skill or activity. My friend teaches a co-op in her home where she teaches cello and her kids learn science and French from the other parents.

Action Tasks

• Research and sign up for extracurricular activities for your children.

HOW TO CREATE HOMESCHOOL SCHEDULE

Start with your monthly schedule

Start with the holidays. What weeks will you need off for holidays for the year? Go ahead and set those aside for the year. I know December can be hectic, so I plan for a very light December schedule and we take two weeks at the end of December, which by mid-year is a welcomed break. Remember to add any other holidays you know you'll take off for the week like at Thanksgiving, March break, or any other holidays you plan on traveling or hosting guests. Don't forget that you'll also need time to prepare, time to pack, or time to ready your home for visitors.

Number of weeks of school

I'm in Ontario so we don't have to keep any records but for those that do, how many hours of school will you need to get in for the year? How many weeks does that correspond to? Will you school through the summer or take it off completely? I plan for 40 weeks of school as our usual school year runs from September to June. Our summer schedule is a lighter schedule filled with fun unit studies and anything that we fall behind with during the year.

Leave room for interruptions

If you know you'll have 40 weeks of school this year and you plan 40 weeks of lessons, it's likely you may get behind and freak out if you're not on track. If I'm planning for 40 weeks of school I'll have 35 weeks of lessons planned. This is because there will be times, other than vacation, that will be lost due to illness, travel or other unexpected events in normal everyday life.

Days on and days off

You may decide that you will only school 4 days a week and have 3 days off or you may want to do six weeks on and one week off. If you run a family business that is seasonal maybe you want to have a lighter homeschool schedule then or not homeschool at all. Each family will have their own schedule they'll need to work around so don't be afraid to step outside of the Monday to Friday routine.

Examine your curriculum

How many lessons does your math book or history curriculum have? How many days will you do that subject each week? Can you get through one lesson in one week or will it take two? Figure this out for each of your books so that you have a rough idea of where you should be in the book.

If you're a paper planner then use pencil, I use my excel sheet to plan our year overview to see if we're on track. If we do get off track I move things to the next week and it's not a big deal.

Be realistic

You don't have to do every subject every day. Be realistic. If you have a newborn, your schedule will look very different from someone that has elementary aged students. If your child will be in competitive swimming, then make sure what you've planned can be catered to your child and their schedule. It's about priorities. You don't want to burn out and you don't want to put unnecessary pressure on your kids to finish the year either.

Homeschooling is a journey and a lifestyle; it won't look the same for everyone so find what works for you and your family.

Action tasks

- Create a monthly schedule to keep you on track for the year.

CREATE A WEEKLY SCHEDULE

Once you've figured out your monthly schedule you might need to break things down by week for yourself and/or your child. A weekly schedule will allow you to see exactly what you can get done each day and how you can tweak your schedule, if needed. If one day runs longer than another, maybe you need to switch some subjects around.

For myself, we do history and science on separate days because they can tend to run long. We always start our day with music and then reading so that we ease into our homeschool day. My younger son's least favorite subject is spelling so he likes to tackle that first. My oldest will begin with math because he needs to be bright and alert to tackle his least favorite subject.

We are not morning people so they like some time to get into their routine.

How many hours of school will you complete each day?

You're not in public school anymore. You will have a lot more one-on-one time with your child, so there's really no need to spend 9am-3pm on school. For us, we've gone one hour for each grade level up to 6 hours for middle school. So my first grader does an hour to two hours of school depending on if we're working on any projects. And that time will increase each year. My 8th grader does 6 hours of school sometimes more if he's dawdling.

What subjects would you like to tackle first? Do you want to do a circle time with the whole family? Do you need a library day or do you have co-op or activities on another?This will let you be able to schedule out your week and see where you can fit school in. You can see my son's 5th grade schedule below.

Weekly Schedule

Tuesday	Wednesday	Thursday	Friday	Saturday
Math (45) ☐	Math (45) ☐	Math (45) ☐	Math (45) ☐	Math (45) ☐
Dictation (15) ☐	Writing (20) ☐	Cursive (10) ☐	Writing (20) ☐	Sci/His Project (1hr) ☐
Grammar (10) ☐	Spelling (15) ☐	Grammar (10) ☐	Spelling (15) ☐	Poetry (15) ☐
Vocab (15) ☐	History (30) ☐	Vocab (15) ☐	History (30) ☐	Art (45) ☐
French (15) ☐	Typing (15) ☐	French (15) ☐	Typing (15) ☐	Music (20) ☐
Science (30) ☐	Reading (1hr) ☐	Science (30) ☐	Reading (1hr) ☐	Reading (1hr) ☐
Reading (1hr) ☐		Reading (1hr) ☐		

Notes: _____
_____
_____

How many days a week will you do school?

If you're schooling year round, perhaps you only want to do school 4 days a week with a library or co-op day on the last day. You'll need to figure out how many hours you need for each subject and go from there.

If your hubby is away part of the weekend and you want to spend time with him while he's home your schedule may be from Tuesday to Saturday. Who said you had to follow the regular school schedule?

Action tasks

- Create a weekly schedule for your family.

To grab the homeschool planning guide printables to help you get started with your plans, visit:

https://www.livinglifeandlearning.com/the-homeschool-planning-guide

---

CREATE A DAILY SCHEDULE THAT WORKS FOR YOU

Do you have a daily schedule for your child or for yourself? This will help you keep your child on track and this will also help them see what is expected of them for the day.

I like writing out my daily schedules because it gives my child and I an idea of his workload for the day. This also eliminates the need to answer the questions, what do I do now/next every 10 minutes from your child. While some may prefer to plan using specific times, this doesn't work for me particularly for the younger ages.

Things do get out of whack and then it bothers me when I get off the schedule, so I like to use a schedule that list subjects in the order they should be completed.

So for my first grader this year, this would be his schedule for Monday:

Music – 30 min
Reading – 30 min
Spelling – 10 min
Math – 20 min
Grammar – 10 min

Writing – 15 min

Science – 30 min

I don't write the time on my son's schedule, but I write out the subjects and add a checkbox that he marks when he is finished. He loves checking the boxes. I print the schedule out onto paper and place it in a sheet protector in his binder. I then write on his schedule with dry erase or wet erase marker. This way it's easy to wipe away and set up the next day.

If you have activities or plans for the day then a timed schedule would be helpful for your child to keep them on track for the day. It also lets them plan ahead.

I like to alternate independent work and teacher intensive work so when you have multiple children, there's time for you to move around to each child and work with them one-on-one. There are your must have subjects that need to be completed each day like math and writing for us, but I alternate the other subjects to give our day some variety and to fit things into our schedule. There's no need to complete all of the subjects every day.

Action tasks

- Create a daily schedule for each child.

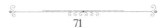

HOW TO PLAN INTEREST LED STUDIES

We've chatted about homeschool curriculum but have you thought about designing your own? Isn't that crazy? You can plan your own. I know, you're thinking, "I'm not a teacher." But you are, and with some planning, you can totally do this.

What are interest-led studies?

Find out where your child's interests lie, and if they don't have one yet, this would be a great time to discover a new passion.

Choose a topic

Ask your child what they would like to study this year. This may surprise you, and it gives them a chance to get involved in their homeschool plans. We started with interest-led studies for science and then worked it in for history too. Take it one step at a time. I'd ask my son what he wanted to study and he said dinosaurs, we studied dinosaurs for a whole year. He still remembers what he learned six years later.

Create an outline

This may seem harder than it is but what I do is take a library book out and look at their table of contents on the subject and figure out from there what topics I'd like to cover in our own studies. It doesn't mean you have to do it all but it gives you a good framework to start.

Find resources

Gather all the resources you'll need like non-fiction and/or fiction books to compose your reading list, activities or projects that will incorporate hands-on learning on the topic, also see if there are any field trips that you can take that would tie in well with your topic. I like searching for printables online to see if anyone has worksheets or their own unit studies. This way I don't have to start everything from scratch.

Find activities

What kind of crafts or projects can you have your child create that would bring this concept alive. My son made his own cuneiform when we were studying ancient Egypt. He loves writing in secret codes and writing in hieroglyphics.

Gather supplies

Create a supplies list of the necessary materials that are needed for each project, then go ahead and purchase everything you need and store it in a box. You'll always have the items on hand for a project and you won't be tempted to skip over it.

Implement your plans

Don't be mad if things don't go as planned, follow those rabbit trails and see where they lead you. It can be as easy as reading books together, writing about what you read, and then creating a craft. Just start, and before you know it, you'll be so deep into your own studies that you won't even need curriculum.

Action tasks

• Choose a topic alongside your child to study and create your own unit study.

CHAPTER 4

GET YOUR HOMESCHOOL ORGANIZED NOW

DIGITAL OR PAPER HOMESCHOOL PLANNER

What kind of planner do you want to use for your homeschool? Do you prefer a binder or a digital planner in a spreadsheet like Excel? There are pros and cons to each but every person has their own preferences and there are so many options now, it's amazing.

I do most of my homeschool planning in an excel spreadsheet set up with the dates of the week on the side and all of my subjects listed across the top. It's super easy to see what I need to do each week and it's also easy to change things around if needed. I haven't found an online program that has met all of my needs and that is simple to use so I don't have any listed here.

Paper Planner

While I love my Excel spreadsheet, nothing beats writing out your plans and then checking them off. I use my Excel sheet to plan my homeschool year, but write out our weekly schedule to keep track of things.

Pros

- can write out plans
- easy to add to
- physical copy of planner
- can check off finished items

Cons

- tedious to write out
- difficult to make changes

Digital planners

Online programs may come with a monthly or yearly fee. If you create your own, this would be the more frugal way to go. It's also a lot easier to customize and make changes as needed. It's also easy to copy and paste material as well.

Pros:

- easy to make changes
- customizable
- free if create your own

Cons:

- need to be on a device

- difficult to locate
- must be printed if want physical copy

Action tasks

- Decide if you'll use a digital or paper planner.

ORGANIZE YOUR HOMESCHOOL SPACE

What if you don't have a homeschool room? I don't have one. We do school in our living room.

Pros: I can watch them as I'm working at the computer, there's plenty of space for all three of my kids at the table, and we're all together.

Cons: if the homeschool is out of order you can't sit in the living room and enjoy it. I need to clean it up or at least shove it back onto the shelves evenly so it's not bothersome. Luckily my youngest is eight now and not a trouble maker, but it could pose a problem if I had a younger child who demanded more attention.

I've homeschooled in a 2 bedroom apartment, a townhouse and our current home, so it can be done no matter where you're living. I find that in smaller spaces, you have to get creative in terms of storage ideas. When we were in the apartment, my linen closet was my book shelves and all of the books I used were in boxes that I could pull out to use with my son. We didn't have any proper book shelves and we used our walk in closet to store our toys. We couldn't use any of those wonderful under the bed storage ideas because our mattresses were on the floor. So if you think you have to be able to afford xyz to homeschool, it can be done super frugally, if needed.

I love the toy bins from Toys "R" Us, I used them to organize my homeschool materials and toys,and they're great for small spaces. I still have them but now also have the 9 cubed shelving unit that we use for toys. I also set up a food store for my daughter so she could use it with her kitchen and for her tea parties.

Organize your books

Have a place for all of your books and curriculum. I have two sets of book shelves on either side of my couch. One side is for curriculum. This is our current curriculum or special things that I may pull out. Previous or next year's curriculum is in a plastic bin in the basement or my second floor storage closet.

The other book shelves hold activities for my youngest to pull out and do on her own. The bottom shelf holds all of our library books and nothing else. I hate hunting down library books only to find that they've been mixed up with our own books, so we try to keep them separated.

Organize your work area

It can be a desk or table or seat on the floor, your child needs a work area of their own, where they can complete their work. This should also house their supplies like pencils, erasers and everything else. I keep this at the computer table along with our printer and laptop. It's a really long table so it houses two computers. This also means they'll have dedicated space to themselves and they'll know where to go once they have to get school started. Of course, my son prefers to be reading his book upside down on the couch while my daughter completes an activity in the middle of the living room floor. I'm just happy that they're getting their work done so it doesn't matter to me where they do it. I keep the younger children with me while my oldest works in the other room so he can focus without his siblings distracting him.

Create a system

Don't fight with constant paper clutter, come up with a system to organize those school papers, art work and assignments so they're not loose and falling all over the place.

Maybe you need an inbox where the day's work is dropped into to be marked and dispersed accordingly. I like to correct everything the same day and have it back in their binders so there's no need for me to hold onto them.

Use spiral notebooks

I got my spiral notebooks at Walmart for five cents when they went on sale in August. I love using them for math, science and history since we do a lot of notebooking and narration. I don't have to deal with loose papers and we don't lose anything.

Organize each subject

For subjects that come with loose paper, or where I create my own activities and to hold notebooking pages, I use a binder and each child has one. Within the binder, I use post it notes to divide up the different subjects in the binders, if I'm using them. Teach them early to place their work in the correct area and to start writing in the proper places. It will save you the headache of helping your child organize their binder after they've crammed 200 pieces of paper in it. Totally been there and it's not fun.

Get the hole reinforcements for paper

With my oldest I have to use a binder because he does a lot of notebooking and uses a lot of printables. I have to buy the hole enforcers to place around the holes of the paper because every time he writes in the binder he pulls the paper away and then it gets ripped out of the binder and I have loose pages everywhere. It takes him an hour to find his assignment he is supposed to be working on from the day before. Hence, get the reinforcements.

Only print what you need

I've made the mistake of printing out a half a year's worth of curriculum, only to find that my child hated it, and we had to switch to something else. Then we ended up with a lot of scrap paper to draw on. Don't be wasteful and only print off a week or two at first to see if it will work. Then maybe a month's worth of work, see how you like it, and then go all out. That way if things change, you're not at a loss.

Organize your shelves

Each child has their own area on my shelves, that way no one loses anything and they all know where everything should go at the end of the day. Make them responsible for their own books and supplies so that when they go missing, there's no one else to blame.

Keep it organized

All the seats around my coffee table have lids and there's storage inside there. I love my table! It currently holds play dough and their toys, dolls, play food and puzzles. There's no way that stuff would fit on my book shelves and I don't want to have to travel upstairs or the basement to get things that they use often.

Each child has their own space on the shelf so if it's messy I know who to call on. They're responsible for their own space and need to help clean up at the end of the day. That way you don't lose your mind trying to do it all and you don't hear complaints because they can't find their pencils.

How to organize school supplies

If you're like me, then we do the bulk of our school shopping during one time of the year and that's during those wonderful back to school sales. For us, here in Ontario, that's August since we go back the day after Labor Day.

This is my Christmas. I love a great school supply deal. I eat them up like a kid in a candy store. My husband just doesn't understand why I'm so giddy about back to school sales. But then again, I could care less about going to the hardware store, so I'm sure we're on the same page.

Find a home for your supplies

I store the bulk of my school supplies like printer paper, notebooks, lined paper in the closet on the second floor. I have baskets filled with pencils, glue sticks and erasers. I only have the things out that I need. On our table there is a bucket which houses our pencils, crayons, and pencil crayons. I also have a hard case that holds more pencils, pens and markers. For some reason, there is never a sharp pencil around which is why I have so many.

My must-have school supplies list

- Printer
- Laptop/computer
- Printer paper
- Lined paper
- Notebooks/duotangs/binders
- Pencils
- Pencil sharpeners
- Erasers
- 3 hole punch

- White glue
- Glue sticks
- Markers
- Colored pencils
- Crayons
- Rulers – I need more than one since they get used as weapons and break
- Pencil case or basket or can to hold supplies

These are my bare necessities, of course if you had book shelves or workboxes and baskets those things would help keep your supplies organized but they are not a necessity.

Use what you have

Most school supplies don't expire. Don't go overboard. Glue sticks, glue and markers may dry out if you have them for a long period of time but the rest you can keep forever. Go through your things before you make your shopping list. There was one year where I only had to buy pencils and erasers because I had so much stuff left over from the previous year. Don't go crazy, remember how we discussed budget, and stick to it.

HOW TO ORGANIZE YOUR AUDIOS AND EBOOKS

What about your digital files like audios and eBooks? You need to have a back-up system to store your files. Especially, if you're like me and love collecting audios and free eBooks. I also buy a lot of digital products to save on shipping to Canada, so my collection is huge. If your computer hard drive dies, you will be heartbroken at the loss of all of your eBooks and files.

I also like to take advantage of the big bundle sales and it's nice to know I have those resources there if needed. But it's no use if I don't know what I have available and if I end up not even using them.

I admit it, I use to be a digital hoarder. I'd go to the homeschool freebie sites and download all the freebies that appeared each day or each week. I'd have an elementary student but download high school resources just in case I needed them later. This left me with a hard drive full of stuff I didn't need. Not to mention they weren't all good resources.

Back up your computer

First and foremost, ensure that you are backing up your computer. There are too many things that are on your computer that you treasure, your pictures, videos and of course your homeschool curriculum, audios and eBooks. You cannot risk losing these. It will cost you a lot of time and effort to try to recover them, and it will be an even bigger nightmare if they're lost. Grab an external hard drive or two, use a cloud service like Dropbox or Drive or burn everything to CDs. I've had a friend that had her external hard drive die, so now she has two. I prefer to use a cloud service so that it syncs to all of my devices.

Track your files

Record what you currently have, I purchased curriculum through an eBook bundle last year and completely forgot what I had available to me this year. It would be a complete waste of money if I didn't use any of it. But that's just our nature, we jump at the sale and then it never gets used because you forget about it. I have since started to keep track of my curriculum and this year, the only thing I had to purchase was half a level of Singapore math and a science workbook to go along with the Apologia book I had borrowed from a friend, something I would never have been able to afford on my own. Considering that I am homeschooling three kids, that's really awesome.

Organize your files

Do not dump all of your resources into a folder named "homeschool." That's what I did my first year and now I can't find anything because there's just so many files to go through. Going forward, I always divide everything into subjects and then seasonal topics, and then by type of resources. So all of my lapbooks are in one place and my notebooking pages are in one place since I use those files the most. I have a folder for science and then subfolders for each area of science like biology and chemistry. I have another one for activities because sometimes I just need a quick and easy project to complete.

Be specific when naming your files

Along with the title of the eBook, I also added grades to them, this makes it super easy to find things when I need something for my 1st grader. I'm a digital file junkie, I collect freebies and store them away because I might need them later on. This is why I need a system.

Use Evernote

This has been the best invention ever. If I find something online that I'd like to read or information that I want to keep for later, I 'clip it' to Evernote. In Evernote, I have a Homeschool Notebook, or folder, where I can store things that I find online. I organized them by subject so it's easy to find later on. It's the perfect tool for digital hoarders. I use this for my business and blog as well. You can take screenshots, write notes, I like to write to-do lists and my shopping list in there because it syncs to my phone as well. I clip all of my recipes there, because even if the site is taken down, you have a digital snapshot of it for your own keeping, and it's free!

Even if you don't use these programs, use a printable for paper and pen lovers or an Excel sheet or Google sheets to keep tabs of your homeschool goodies, but whatever you do, keep track of what you have on hand. It's a great way to save money and put it to good use. It's no good to anyone if you don't use it.

Action Task

- Take a digital inventory of your homeschool curriculum, eBooks and audio files.

To grab the homeschool planning guide printables to help you get started with your plans, visit:

https://www.livinglifeandlearning.com/the-homeschool-planning-guide

CHAPTER 5

WAYS TO KEEP YOUR HOMESCHOOL RUNNING SMOOTHLY

WHEN THINGS DON'T GO AS PLANNED

So you've created these amazing plans, what happens when or if they get shattered? What happens when they get thrown out the window? It does and can happen. You've picked out the perfect curriculum but your kids are less than enthusiastic about it.

No matter how much research you do, the curriculum you choose may not be a good fit for your family after you've used it for two weeks. Or you signed them up for an activity and now they've decided they hate it. What do you do?

Breathe

Just breathe, homeschool plans can fall through, it can and will happen to you. Don't fret, take a breather, have some chocolate. You are not alone.

You've purchased an expensive curriculum that you just hate, now what? See how you can turn it into a blessing, sell it, expensive curriculum usually has a higher used price tag so see if you can recoup some of that loss. It's no one's fault, don't take it out on your child. Homeschooling can be a trial and error process, you just have to figure out what works for you as a family.

Take a break

Lay off the curriculum and enjoy some reading, get writing done by using copywork from their favorite books, or watch a ton of documentaries, head outdoors and go on a nature walk.

Add something fun

Do something fun, a messy project or a field trip. Remember that learning doesn't always have to take place in books. Get outside and explore. If they have a great new interest, turn it into a unit study and get them to research it and do a presentation.

New plans

Yes, you will need to create new homeschool plans, it's a part of the process, and you've now discovered something that doesn't work for your family, it's one more thing to stay away from. Celebrate the fact that you get to look for something else and open your eyes to new ways of learning.

HOW TO EVALUATE WHAT IS WORKING IN YOUR HOMESCHOOL

What happens after you've gone through all this planning and you find it isn't working with your kids. What do you do if it just doesn't work for you? You can have the best plans laid out on paper, or computer, but you won't know ifit'll work until you try it out with your kids. Someone may not want to do the math curriculum you picked out or perhaps they hate the soccer class you've signed up for. You can have the best plans, but if it doesn't work for your kids, you need to be able to recognize when you may need to make a change.

Let me tell you, however you imagined your kids and your homeschool at the start of this journey, it's not going to look like that. You know that image that you have of reading to your child as you're snuggled up on the couch with them hanging onto your every word? That doesn't happen here. One child is doodling, the other one wants to chew on the book, and the other child is trying to read another book because your book is not interesting enough. That is my house.

Things will not be perfect, you will not be able to check off everything on your to-do list, every single day. There will be good days and there will be bad ones. But how can you tell if it's something that has to change with you or your curriculum?

Are there tears?

If there are tears about homeschooling there are issues that will need to be addressed first. I think particularly when you are bringing home a child from public school, there's a resistance to seeing you as a teacher. This means you get more defiant behavior toward school and not wanting to do the work or being argumentative. Homeschooling is a lifestyle and it will need a period of adjustment.

However, sometimes it's the curriculum and it doesn't jive or it's just too hard and the level is not appropriate. I think it's easy to get caught up in grade levels and you really have to meet your child where they are at and go from there. That's why I'm not a fan of all in one packaged curricula because a child may on grade level for math but need more help with spelling.

Is it your expectations?

Are they too high? If you've set your own expectation without evaluating how things are working for your child or that they may have differing needs, they'll always fail to meet your expectations. Then you feel disappointment and if your child senses this, it can be a loss for everyone. Are your expectations appropriate? I love setting goals with my kids so that they can gain their own sense of achievement as they work towards accomplishing them.

Have you found your groove?

Have you found your homeschooling groove where things are, for the most part, sailing smoothly? If there are hiccups in your schedule, don't be afraid to move things around. I found that when my son was taking judo, it worked best if we dedicated that day to running errands and the library. Once we returned home, there wasn't a lot of school work being done. We were still getting school done but no one was in the mood for seat work which was fine with me.

If it works then no need to change anything. When you go messing with things that are not broken, that's when you start to break things.

Is the grass greener elsewhere?

I know I've experience this myself, I'll be reading online or talking with another homeschool mom about a new curriculum they're using and loving, and I start to question my own decisions.

Maybe I need to try this brand new thing because it's bright and shiny. I always end up regretting it because it doesn't work for us and it's a waste of money. When you're new you think you're missing out on everything else. Now that I've found what works for us, I don't have to change anything because I know what works.

Change is good

Things are not set in stone; you have the freedom to change things up as needed. You don't have to school from Monday to Friday, 9am to 3pm. When my husband worked weekends, we did school from Wednesday to Sunday and in the afternoons. That's just what worked for us. You're not doing school at home, but you are implementing learning into your regular routine. Make it fun and do what works for you.

Action Tasks

- Use the checklist to evaluate your homeschool.

5 WAYS TO TELL THAT YOU ARE DOING TOO MUCH IN YOUR HOMESCHOOL

You have your curriculum and your homeschool schedule but it's also easy to over schedule your kids and plan too much. But just because you've created plans, doesn't mean they are going to be perfect. When you jump into homeschooling, it's easy to sign up for too many activities outside of the home which can bring stress to you and your family.

Are you feeling overwhelmed?

Do you take a look at your week and just feel tired from looking at it? Do you find yourself feeling overwhelmed when you haven't even started your day? Or perhaps you are always rushing your child onto the next thing in order to finish everything in your plans. If there are too many outside activities, you may want to consider cutting back on those for a term to see which one should be made a priority and which ones can be put off to another term.

Are your children overtired?

Do you have meltdowns in the middle of the day that don't

have to do with food? Is your child combative or more defiant then they usually are? Maybe they're not getting enough sleep and running around from activity to activity is making them feel overtired. Perhaps your child is more pleasant on the weekends when things don't move at such a fast pace. Ensure that your child is getting at least 8 hours of sleep or more depending on their age.

Has your child started slacking in school?

Related to the last point, if they are overtired you'll see this manifest in their schooling. Are they not trying as hard or complaining about the workload that they are usually able to manage? If their schedule is crammed with schoolwork and extra-curricular activities, you'll need to evaluate what should be a priority in your child's life. Can they give up on one activity or take a break from it?

Does your child have free time?

What does your child do for fun? There should be time in your child's day for them to relax and choose to do something of their choosing and I don't mean a program or activity they've signed up for. I mean do they have time to draw, create or build? A creative outlet that doesn't have any limits but their imagination, they need time to develop their passions. Is there time in their day for them to get outside and just be kids, play with their friends or ride their bike? We spend so much time thinking they need this activity or these lessons to be a great adult, but play is important as well.

Do you have time together as a family?

If there isn't time in your day to sit down together to read or talk then you have a problem. If your family's schedule is too crazy that you don't have time to spend quality time together then please evaluate what you can let go of to make this happen. Don't spend your time shuffling from one activity to another. Read, play and build together so that those are the memories that will stick in your child's mind.

HOW TO TEACH MULTIPLE KIDS

When you have two or more kids, homeschool scheduling can get a bit more complicated. You have to ensure that your schedule works for your child's level of independence. You will be spending more time with the younger children while older children can work more independently. Reading and music lessons are perfect examples of independent activities that a child could do on their own, if they can read.

Intersperse independent work with teaching subjects

Subjects that require more mom time will need to have the other children doing less teacher intensive subjects while you work with that one child. Or else you have one child waiting for you while you're working with another, and if they're waiting on you, it's more likely that they'll wander off or start bothering their siblings, so I want to keep them in "school mode." While one child is completing their music lesson, you could be working with another on their math, while an older child starts their writing program. For subjects that require a skill such as reading, math, and writing, you'll have to schedule individual time with the child unless you are using a computer based curriculum, then you can be more hands off.

For content areas like history and science, you can bring everything together but have more detailed work for older children. Little ones can sit in on the lesson and watch or create their own crafts or projects, but you could require a written summary or narration from older children, they could also research deeper into the topic and write a report for you as well.

Work with the littles ones first

I always find that the little ones will keep themselves better occupied on their own when they've had some good one-on-one mommy time. By reading, singing and playing together they get their mommy fill and then they are ready to go play on their own. With babies, it's best to wear them, it keeps your hands free to work with your kids and you get baby cuddling time at the same time. The next section will focus on ideas for the little ones.

Get the older child to occupy younger students

Pair up your little one with another child and have them spend time with their sibling while you work with another. This way your little one isn't left out and they get some sibling time together. Depending on the child's age, you could even have them teach the younger child. Reading and playing games can be a wonderful way to spend time together while not getting riled up during school.

Make a visible schedule

Get your children on a schedule. Create a visible schedule with large images so your little knows what will happen and when. You can add in snack and meal times, outside and nap times, so they will learn to transition easier from one activity to the next. Every child needs to have their own schedule, whether it's a giant poster board on the wall or a printed schedule for each child in their binder, find a system that will work for your family and keep you sane.

HOW TO OCCUPY THE LITTLE ONES WHILE YOU TEACH

If you have a baby or toddler in your family, little ones can definitely make things more challenging as you try to homeschool the older children. With little ones around, your most productive time will be nap time. I use this time to do the more focused work with the older kids, so I'm not worrying about what they're getting into. With my oldest, it was math time and with my younger son, we did his school work during my daughter's entire nap time since he was only in kindergarten/grade 1 at the time.

Create your own busy bags or quiet boxes

Prepare activities ahead of time that your toddler can use during the school time that will keep them busy. These can be kept in large Ziploc bags or if you have the space, storage boxes.

Busy bag suggestions:

- Paper and stickers
- Paper with cut up shapes of construction paper and glue
- Coloring pages with crayons
- Strips of paper and scissors (if they're ready)
- Play dough and tools

- Blocks
- Cars with a road mat
- Felt story boards

You can find more preschool ideas on my website - LivingLifeandLearning.com.

Rotate toys

I'm sure your home is filled with a ton of children's toys from aunts, uncles and grandparents. Tuck some of them away and rotate the toys that are available for your children to play with. I know that my kids will play with a toy for a period of time, and then forget about them. Then when they find it again, it's like a brand new toy.

Have special school only toys or activities that can only be used during school time so that they don't lose their appeal and have your little ones excited about school time. I know a mother of 10 who said she would just layout a roll of butcher paper and all the little kids would spend their time drawing and coloring.

Action tasks

- Prepare activities for your little ones.

HOW TO AVOID HOMESCHOOL BURNOUT

During or nearing the end of the school year, you've played the role of your child's teacher but you long for those simpler days where you could just be their mother and not worry about school. You begin to feel burnt out, and that my friends is what homeschool burnout is. That feeling that you'd rather clean your washrooms and pantry then try to get the kids to do school. Then you put on some documentaries and have them help you cook and call it school for the day.

It happens to the best of us and I went through it last year. You never get to hang up that teacher hat because you are now responsible for your child's education. How do you feel when you absolutely have to do something you don't want to do? You find everything in your power to not do it. You do laundry, you start knitting, and you clean out that hallway closet that no one ever touches. It can get bad and I have been there.

Last year, we had some struggles and I just wanted to push through it all. At the end of the year, I did not want to touch another school book until the fall. This is a departure from the homeschooling through the summer that we usually do. When September started, it was horrendous trying to get everyone back on schedule and back into the routine of completing school work. I completely regretted taking the summer off.

What I found was that because I was pushing through I wasn't making school fun anymore and the kids resisted. Not that all school work has to be fun, but I was definitely more uptight in terms of our schedule. I was constantly saying, let's hurry up and finish so we can do the next thing, and it wasn't fun anymore. I was a drill sergeant and I didn't like what I had become.

Then I just didn't want to do any of it and we took the summer off. It can happen during the year or at the end. I know around December I feel like we're stuck in our daily routine so we change things up with fun Christmas activities and bake cookies. A part of it is knowing what are your triggers are, then knowing how to alleviate them.

Plan ahead

If you know you're going to be super busy in December then plan ahead and have some fun projects ready that you can complete or books that fit the season to read together and evaluate. Maybe you need to take more breaks with a longer school year. You can change things up if you find yourself in that homeschool rut.

Take time for yourself

When was the last time you did something for yourself? Alone. Yeah, me neither. Maybe you just need to enjoy a sappy love story movie and cry it out with some chocolate. When you make time for yourself it doesn't have to be some extravagant stay at a five star hotel. It may just be coffee with another mom.

Ask for help when needed

Do you need help with housework or with the kids? Maybe you can hire a teen to be a mother's helper for an afternoon or two while you run errands or get some housework done. Or if you have a friend with the same age kids, you could trade play dates to get stuff done while your kids are playing with their friends.

Give yourself permission to let things go

You can't do it all and no one should expect you to. Can your spouse teach a subject, can your trade off with another homeschool mother, or even start your own co-op with a few homeschooling families.

You can't expect to keep every aspect of your life in perfect order. Dishes will pile up, school work may be missed, you may feel exhausted, it's normal and you have to learn what you need to prioritize and what you need.

CHAPTER 6

TIPS TO MAINTAIN YOUR MOM SANITY

5 MEAL PLANNING TIPS

So as homeschool mothers, not only do you have to teach your children, they always seem to get hungry. You're responsible for feeding everyone as well, which doesn't have to be a huge chore if you put some planning into it.

So, why are we discussing meal planning if we're discussing homeschool planning? Well, if you don't have your meals planned out, you spend more and then don't have any money left over to buy books. If it were up to me, I'd buy books first and think of groceries after. I love my books.

We all know that meals go along with homeschools because as mothers, we need to feed our kids and take care of the house as well.

Make a list

As simple as it sounds, you need to make a list. Go through your flyers to check out sales, what should you look for and what is on sale? What meals can you make from that? Don't just make the list, actually stick to it while you are shopping. Or else your budget gets out of whack and there goes your book money, noooo!

Shop for in season items

Seasonal produce is cheaper, look for items that are on sale and see if they can be substituted into your regular meals or better yet, try a new recipe and use those new veggies. If it's not on sale, I'm not buying it.

Quick meals during the week

If your family is out all day with co-op or activities, invest in a slow cooker. You can throw all of your ingredients in the slow cooker in the morning and you'll have a deliciously tender meal waiting for you when you get home. I also like to cook a double portion of say soup or stew and have it for two nights. The kids and my husband don't mind and it saves me from having to cook the next day.

I save my more intensive prep time meals for the weekends when my husband can watch the kids and keep them. I spend my weekends cutting and seasoning meat for the week. I also cook more time intensive meals on the weekend.

Use your left overs

If you had a rotisserie chicken for dinner, use the left overs for sandwiches the next day, don't let food go to waste. You could also use the carcass to create a wonderful chicken broth. If you're going to make lasagna, then use the extra meat and sauce to make pasta another night of the week.

Meal prep after you shop

Don't throw that tray of chicken breasts right into the freezer. It will take hours to thaw and add too much time to your weekday cooking sessions. Divide up the meat, portion them out and season them now, then throw them in the freezer. Have you seen the Chicken and Beef Dump Recipes from Sharla on The Chaos and the Clutter? It's so easy to put together and you'll have amazing meals throughout the week with very little prep time.

Action tasks

- Create a meal plan for the upcoming week or month.

A CLEANING SCHEDULE THAT WON'T KILL YOU

Cleaning is the last thing that I want to get done on my to-do list, I will admit that. It's my least favorite thing to do but the thing I do first to get it out of the way.

Quick pick ups

I hate spending hours cleaning so I prefer to work in shorter bursts. Each day I dedicate a day of the week to a different area of the home and rotate so that each room gets touched at least once each week. I'm not talking about sparkling shining from floor to ceiling but even if you spend ten minutes in one room, you'd be amazed at how much better it looks after you're done.

Get into a routine

I do laundry two days a week and one or two loads each time. I don't let it pile up into a mountain before I attack because then it becomes overwhelming. I do think my kids can wear a shirt more than one day before it gets washed, well, except for my teen. I'm not washing it just because it touched them. However, once there are stains or noticeable smells, they get washed.

I wash my floors once a week and I vacuum every night, it has to be done, we have a dog so it's just not possible to skip that without having pet hair everywhere. Find your rhythm and get in your groove.

Monthly deep cleanses

Spend a day doing all of the longer deep cleaning items like cleaning the fridge, washing the walls or dusting in those unreachable places. Get into the habit of writing down what you need to get done and the last time you touched it.

You know that horrible mountain of junk mail or important papers, do you have a system in place to deal with them? If you need to keep it, put it away. If you don't need it, into the garbage it goes right away, not stored and hung onto for two months before it goes into the garbage.

Delegate the work

Work with your family to get your cleaning list completed. Your children can help you get a lot done, it doesn't all have to be on you. If you have older children they can take on more responsibility and you can find simple tasks for little ones to help with as well. My 4 year old loves helping me sweep in the kitchen. Does she do a perfect job? No, but she's learning to help mama and feels responsible for getting that task done. She loves folding her own laundry and always keeps her own clothes neatly folded and put away. None of my boys cared for that but they still had to help. They're responsible for their own toys, they keep their own rooms clean and they help their sister clean up her mess too. My teenager mows the lawn and takes care of the garbage, he vacuums daily and does the book shelf dusting. My younger son handles all of the toys that he and his sister bring out during the day. Each of the boys are responsible for one of the bathrooms, this has been a huge help since it needs daily cleaning. Because they're cleaning the bathrooms, they have a better appreciation for keeping it clean. They do a quick wipe down while I do the deeper cleaning weekly.

Work out what you need to do and what your spouse will take care. I don't touch anything that's in the garage where he has all his tools and car stuff. That's his department but the garden shed is mine because I'm the one using it.

If you need help ask for it, you'd be surprised at how much help you may receive from family or friends or your own children.

Action tasks

- Create a cleaning schedule for you and your kids.

7 TIME MANAGEMENT TIPS

How many times have you told someone you homeschool and they look at you like you're a saint and tell you they could never do that? How can you find the time to do it all? You may work outside of the home, or may be a work-at-home-mom like me. How can you be sure to find the time to get it all done without sacrificing time with your children?

It's all a balancing game. What can be sacrificed and what needs your attention right now? That crying baby is usually at the top of that priority list. Each parent will have their own priorities lists and you need to create one first. What do you need to get done each day, what should get done, and then what can be worked on if you have time.

Create boundaries

Ensure that you create boundaries for yourself, your work, and your homeschool. Don't stay up late planning or on social media. If you wake up tired and miserable, no one is going to have a good day. Realize that you need to be on point for everything to go smoothly. Take care of yourself. By creating boundaries you're putting yourself right on up there on the priorities list along with your kids.

Do you really need to schedule a playdate after the kids have been to swimming and piano lessons? Do you absolutely have to answer the phone in the midst of a math lesson? It can wait.

Create a daily to-do list

Use an app, planner or sticky note, what is your to-do list for today? Write it all down including your cleaning task, outings and such so you don't forget anything. Then attack the most difficult tasks first. If you leave them last on your list, it's likely that they won't get done. Get it over with and get the hardest, most unwanted things out of the way first. Then when it comes to the easy tasks, you can easily tackle those no problem.

FOCUS ON YOUR PRIORITIES

What needs to happen now versus later? Email and social media can wait, get the kids on their way with school and use those quiet afternoon times for your work as your sit alongside your child. If not, you may have to leave it for the evening when the kids have settled in. I know I can't get any writing done during the day, so I work on other tasks during the day and save my writing for when the kids are in bed.

For tasks that require my full attention, I know I can't get them done with three kids pulling in every direction so I know they have to wait until they're in bed or I need to get up before they do in the morning to get some work done.

They are my priorities but I know sometimes those lines get blurred and I mix work and parenting and it always leaves me feeling guilty so I strive to do as I say and practice it daily.

Get organized

Ensure that you have a plan for your meals the next day so you're not scrambling around the kitchen trying to figure out what you'll be making the next day. You can thaw meat, cut up vegetables or pack lunch if you'll be out for the day. Leave your homeschool room organized at the end of each day so that you are not searching for things when you start up the next day. Teach the kids to put their own belongings away. Make sure there is a place for everything and that everyone knows where things belong so it doesn't always fall all on you to maintain the school room, especially if you have older children. Younger kids can still help and my four year old has her own cubby where she stores her books and supplies and it's at her level so she's able to clean up herself.

Eliminate electronics

It can be a huge time suck to constantly be checking email or social media, you really need to ensure that you've placed limits on your electronics usage. Set an example for your kids. It's so easy to sit at the computer and come off hours later only to realize that you haven't completed anything on your to-do list.

Set a timer

If you have a task to complete, set the timer for the allotted time and work to complete it by the alarm. This pushes you to be more productive and avoid things that suck up your time. When I work on the computer I use the Chrome app: Strict Workflow, I added all of my social media sites and email addresses to it.

I work for 25 minutes and then I'm locked out of all of those sites. This gives me 25 minutes of concentrated work and then you get 5 minutes of access to all of those sites. This is the best invention ever. I have my son use this as well so that he's not tempted to go wondering around YouTube when he knows he should be getting his work done on the computer.

Get the kids involved

You are not alone in your home. Get your kids involved with the meal prep and clean up. All of the kids have zones that they are responsible for so when it needs to be cleaned up, I know who to turn to. Older children get more responsibilities but that doesn't mean your littles should be left out. They too can have little jobs to help you out around the house. My 4 year old loves sweeping and helping mama in the kitchen. She also puts all the utensils from the dishwasher away.

HOW TO KEEP YOUR SANITY

As a mother, you will have times that you doubt yourself and wonder if you are truly doing the best thing for your family by homeschooling them. It's so easy to get plagued by doubts and fears. By the end of the year, you may even start to get burnt out. What you can do to keep your sanity? A well planned homeschool is the first step but that isn't all.

We are more than homeschool teachers, we are mothers, wives and woman. It's not the only thing that we have going on in our lives. Homeschooling can feel like a huge burden, so you have to ensure that you are taking care of yourself. Self-care is more difficult if you don't recognize that you actually need it.

Make friends

I mean friends for yourself. It's great to connect with other homeschooling mothers to share your insecurities and ask questions. Other people just don't get what you're going through as a homeschool mom and it's nice to have someone to bounce ideas off of as well.

Get healthy

Take the kids out, don't be trapped in your home, get some fresh air and get some physical activity. I'm sure you've worried about your kids health but have you look at your own? Do you drink eight glasses of water daily, exercise or get enough sleep? Don't forget about yourself.

I know I would always insist on the kids eating their veggies, but for my meals I would nitpick at the leftovers. If you're asking your kids to eat their veggies, make sure you're doing the same. They need their mother, and one that is plagued by fatigue and health issues is no fun.

Are you staying up late binge watching a TV show on Netflix? Maybe that can wait while you get your much needed eight hours of sleep. We all know anything can happen at night, a baby starts shrieking, someone has wet their bed, nightmares are plaguing another child, you never know so be prepared to tackle the next day with some sleep rather than none.

Trade babysitting duties

By making new friends, you can see if they'd like to trade babysitting duties so that you can run your errands and get some housework done without kids screaming everywhere. Or use it to take a breather and some time for yourself. I've done this with friends, if they need some time to prep for a trip or have to take another child to an appointment, they'll drop off their child here to hang out with my kids. The kids love it. It's a win-win for everyone.

Take a day for yourself

Give yourself permission to take a day for yourself, to go shopping or do whatever it is that you really would like to do that you can't often do during those homeschooling hours. Sit in your bathtub and read a book, or head to the YMCA and burn off some steam. Hangout with your girlfriend, without the kids, so you can just catch up. Have a date night with your hubby, when was the last time that happened? Make it happen, schedule it into your calendar right now. And if you can't get away, schedule time for you to do something you love, sit back and enjoy a sappy love movie, whatever helps you relieve some stress.

Find a hobby

Take your mind off of homeschooling, and see what other passions you can awaken. When your kids see you learning new things or enjoying your own hobby this will help them discover their own passions and work toward one of their goals.

Find quiet time for yourself

At the end of the day, or before the kids are awake, find some time where you can unwind with a good book or just relax and not have to worry about homeschooling, or the kids, or the house. Take some time to mentally block all of those things out so you can come back the next day rejuvenated. This may be a great time for you to read the bible or enjoy a good book before you get pulled into the needs of the day or so you can relax before bed.

Action Tasks

- Schedule time for yourself today and write it down.

HOW TO BE A MOM AND A TEACHER

Becoming a homeschooling mother takes a bit of time to get used to, especially if you're bringing your child home from public school. They may need time to need time to adapt. They may not be used to you as the teacher. I think it's a role that needs to be eased into. Each year I start our school off the same way. We start with one or two subjects for a couple days and every few days I add in more subjects. I don't start homeschooling eight hour days straight out of the gate. The kids would mutiny.

Don't they always say that your kids always listen to other adults better than they do to you? I've been telling my son that he needs to floss because he had a dentist appointment coming up. I kept hearing, "But why?" and he did not take it seriously because of course mom doesn't know anything. Well, he went to the dentist and was told by the hygienist and dentist that he needed to work on his brushing and flossing. Now, he's in the bathroom working on it with rigor.

Slowly build up to your full-time homeschool schedule. It doesn't have to be all or nothing.

Be prepared that it won't be all sunshine and rainbows

I know when I started that I had pictured homeschooling as all sunshine and rainbows and it was anything but. I never knew how my patience could be tested, how I could be tested as a homeschool teacher, or as a mother. I found myself getting frustrated because my kids were not getting it. This affected how I spoke to them because my expectations were not in line with their abilities. This caused havoc in our homeschool. Had I just met them at their level and built them up from there, it would have gone more smoothly.

Homeschooling will test your will as a mother and you have to decide if it will bend. It won't always be easy and you will have to adapt and change what you know to make things work but the rewards are far greater than anything you've done. When my son was in the first grade at public school, I felt like we never had time together because we hurried to get him to school and then after school we raced through dinner then getting ready for the next school day. There weren't any hours in the day left for just us. Now I'm home with them all the time and it's such a blessing, even though I may not always feel that way. On those days that run long or something is not working. I wouldn't trade it in for the world.

Know when to put on your mom hat

Because I'm their teacher, sometimes I forget that I'm also their mother, and you need to put away that teacher hat and just wear the mom hat. I don't want school issues to permeate into other areas of our family relationship but sometimes it's hard to let things go. Sometimes you just have to push forward and be the one they cry to about school without being offended by their comments, really listen to their needs and be their mom. Remember that fun mom that didn't have to worry about school and just enjoyed being with them, that one. You're a homeschooler and a mom and switching between the two can be hard but is sometimes needed to nurture them.

You're doing this, you get to be one of those awesome homeschool families, and you're really doing it. Don't spend your time planning every single minute of it and rushing through it shuffling your child from one thing to the next one. Enjoy it. Sit back and enjoy those books you'll read together or those messy projects you'll get to jump into. You can do this and it all starts with a plan but it surely does not end there.

ABOUT THE AUTHOR

Monique helps overwhelmed moms who homeschool by giving them a simple, step by step plan so they feel confident their kids are learning, they know how to create their own fun lessons, and so they find joy in homeschooling with less stress.

Monique is the creator of Living Life and Learning where she shares math and science resources for preschool and elementary homeschooling families.

She has a Masters of Science Degree in Biology, has homeschooled her 3 kids for 11 years in Ontario Canada, and mostly survives on coffee and dark chocolate.

To connect with Monique and get more resources, visit: https://www.livinglifeandlearning.com/about

Grab the homeschool planning guide printables to help you get started with your homeschool plans right away, visit:

https://www.livinglifeandlearning.com/the-homeschool-planning-guide.

CPSIA information can be obtained
at www.ICGtesting.com
Printed in the USA
LVHW100205120423
744141LV00006B/273